Tribal Law and Order Act: Five Years Later: How have the Justice Systems in Indian Country Improved?

United States Senate Committee on Indian Affairs

December 2, 2015

ISBN-10   1533115249

ISBN-13   978-1533115249

Table of Contents

Testimony of

Lawrence S. Roberts

Principal Deputy Assistant Secretary for Indian Affairs

United States Department of the Interior

Hearing on

Tribal Law and Order Act: Five Years Later: How have the Justice
Systems in Indian Country Improved?

December 2, 2015

Chairman Barrasso, Vice-Chairman Tester, and members of the
Committee, my name is Lawrence Roberts and I am the Principal Deputy
Assistant Secretary of Indian Affairs at the Department of the Interior
(Department). Thank you for the opportunity to provide testimony before
this Committee on the Tribal Law and Order Act (TLOA), Pub. L. No. 111-
211 (2010). On July 29, 2010, President Obama signed TLOA into law
with the goal of improving public safety in Indian Country. I am pleased
to be here before this Committee today, more than five years after the
law's enactment, to provide an update on the Bureau of Indian Affairs
Office of Justice Services (BIA-OJS) work with Tribes to implement TLOA.

The health, welfare, and safety of our Tribal communities are priorities of
the Obama Administration. TLOA has provided Tribes additional resources

and has fostered greater self-determination and self-governance of their justice systems. Law enforcement and public safety in the United States is largely administered on a local level and TLOA has helped ensure that this is also the situation in Indian Country.

Indian Country still faces many public safety challenges. As the Committee knows, far too many tribal communities are experiencing the devastating effects of alcohol and drugs. However, the Administration is encouraged by the progress made and believes that public safety has and will continue to improve in Indian Country. Updates on implementation and other related services follow.

Law Enforcement Training Standards

TLOA promoted greater flexibility in training law enforcement officers patrolling Indian Country. TLOA provided that law enforcement training standards could be satisfied through training at a State or tribal police academy, a State, regional, local, or tribal college or university, or other training academy that met appropriate standards. BIA-OJS has responded by permitting greater flexibility in training of police officers serving Indian Country. Five years later, training of law enforcement officers in Indian country is more flexible which results in a larger pool of eligible applicants and a better trained workforce.

The Indian Police Academy developed the three-week "Basic Police Officer Bridge Training Program" to meet relevant federal training standards for state trained officers serving Indian Country. The bridge program offers federal law and BIA-OJS policy courses including training on jurisdiction in Indian Country and TLOA. State-trained officers submit a basic training waiver to the academy for review and approval for reciprocity of minimum training standards. Approved training allows applicants to attend the basic bridge program instead of the fifteen-week basic police program. To date, the Indian Police Academy has provided ten sessions of the three-week "Basic Police Officer Bridge Training Program" and has trained 108 law enforcement officers in the program. Overall, the program has an 89 percent graduation rate.

Section 231(b) of TLOA provided that BIA-OJS develop policies and procedures to enter into deputation agreements for the purpose of issuing BIA Special Law Enforcement Commissions (SLECs). SLECs allow full time certified Tribal, Federal, state, and local enforcement officers to assist BIA in the enforcement of Federal criminal statues in Indian

Country. These policies and procedures were developed and enacted on January 25, 2011. Additionally in 2011, BIA-OJS and DOJ partnered to update the Criminal Jurisdiction in Indian Country (CJIC) training curriculum. The course was completely redesigned to provide current information on law enforcement, jurisdiction and legal topics; all of which are critical to the successful response, investigation and prosecution of federal crimes in Indian Country. The new two and half day CJIC training curriculum was piloted in Oklahoma in March 2012, followed by a subsequent pilot in California in April 2012 based on fine-tuning revisions. The standard CJIC curriculum was then rolled out nationwide.

The course is taught by Indian Country AUSAs and Tribal Liaisons from DOJ. This is consistent with TLOA's provisions regarding the duties of Assistant United States Attorney Tribal Liaisons, including: "Conducting training sessions and seminars to certify special law enforcement commissions to tribal justice officials and other individuals and entities responsible for responding to Indian country crimes." The CJIC curriculum and materials were disseminated to the United States Attorney Offices with Indian Country in their jurisdiction for familiarization, since their personnel serve as the actual course instructors. DOJ also reviews the

CJIC course curriculum and materials annually, updating legal issues and case law.

In 2015, BIA-OJS and DOJ collaborated to create and implement a CJIC Master Schedule approach by disseminating a CJIC training schedule for the upcoming year, including locations and dates. This allows for advance planning by all agencies involved, including law enforcement partners that require training and DOJ Indian Country AUSAs and Tribal Liaisons within the various districts.

BIA-OJS also assists Tribes with background checks during the hiring process of tribal law enforcement officers. Section 231(a)(4)(A) requires BIA-OJS, when requested by a Tribe, to conduct background checks for tribal law enforcement and correctional officials no later than 60 days after the date of receipt of the request. BIA-OJS has developed a new background policy and provided background and adjudication training throughout the country. During FY 2015 OJS provided a total of fifty-eight (58) background investigation for twenty-eight (28) tribes.

Data/Information Sharing

TLOA recognized that accurate data is essential for the development of effective public safety strategies. It also recognized that data is a fundamental tool of law enforcement and the need to share such data among law enforcement agencies. TLOA addressed this issue in a variety of ways. It provided for BIA-OJS to share with DOJ all relevant crime data received from tribal law enforcement agencies. BIA-OJS has accomplished this requirement. Today, Tribes and BIA agencies provide data to the FBI's Uniform Crime Report (UCR) data collection process through electronic submissions. BIA-OJS took a lead role in achieving a seamless transition for Indian Country. BIA-OJS coordinated multiple training sessions for tribes and BIA agencies on the FBI's UCR Program. Furthermore, BIA-OJS followed up with individual technical assistance and additional training to ensure that deployment of the electronic reporting was a success for Tribes.

Further, Section 211(b)(2)(D)(13) provided for BIA-OJS to provide technical assistance and training to tribal law enforcement officials to gain access and input authority to utilize the National Criminal Information Center and other national crime information databases. BIA-OJS has been working with DOJ to identify needs in Indian Country regarding access to databases with the FBI's Criminal Justice Information Services (CJIS) Division. BIA-OJS has engaged directly with tribal leaders to discuss their needs and provide information on CJIS programs.

There have been a number of successes in implementing the TLOA information sharing provisions. For example, the Sycuan Tribal Police Department's officers, all of whom are commissioned by the Bureau of Indian Affairs-Office of Justice Services (BIA) as special deputy officers, were approved to access the state's robust law enforcement telecommunications system, CLETS — a first in the state of California. In FY 2015, BIA-OJS received authority to perform name-based, emergency background checks for tribal social service entities that require such information for child placement purposes, via federal criminal databases housed within the FBI's CJIS Division. BIA-OJS is piloting a project wherein tribes may contact BIA-OJS to obtain name based criminal history information in exigent circumstances where a fingerprint based check is not feasible.

Section 211(b)(2)(D)(10) provided for BIA-OJS to develop and provide dispatch and emergency and E-911 services. BIA-OJS has procured state of the art dispatch equipment to integrate communications systems and record radio and telephone traffic at 17 direct service agencies. Five agencies will be complete by calendar year end with remainder complete in calendar 2016. Technical assistance is also provided to tribes, when requested, for dispatch, coverage and equipment requirements. BIA-OJS also provides tribes with technical assistance in acquiring frequencies for tribally operated and owned systems.

Finally, section 211 of TLOA provided for BIA-OJS to develop an annual report of unmet staffing needs of the law enforcement, corrections, and tribal court programs. In April of 2013 BIA-OJS submitted a report to Congress detailing the allocation and expenditure of FY 2010 funds appropriated to the BIA for public safety and justice programs, as well as the estimated unmet needs for public safety and justice programs. The scope of the April 2013 report was limited to tribes providing public safety funding by BIA and agency office locations that expended public safety and justice funds to provide direct services to tribes. The Department is providing a comprehensive update to the April 2013 report which is in the final stages of departmental review. Section 211 also provided for BIA-OJS to report on: "the formula, priority list or other methodology used to determine the method of disbursement of funds for the public safety and justice programs administered by the Office of Justice Service." To address this part of TLOA, a description of the BIA-OJS funding methodology was incorporated into the FY 2016 President's Budget Request. Since the beginning of the Obama Administration in FY 2008, just over $100 million in BIA public safety appropriation increases have been allocated using this methodology and the resulting impact on violent crime in Indian Country shows that with increased resources Tribes are able to better protect their communities. Applying programmatic expertise and data-driven analysis, our distribution method enables BIA to target additional resources to reservations with higher violent crime rates and larger service populations, indicators of the severity of public safety needs. Additionally, BIA-OJS is currently discussing the viability of a tribal advisory group. The advisory group would focus on public safety and tribal justice funding, and seek tribal perspectives on current funding distribution methods.

Tribal Courts

BIA-OJS has focused on strengthening Tribal Courts through a number of different initiatives. TLOA amended the Tribal Justice Support Act which now identifies funding for specific tribal court personnel positions through Tribal Justice Systems appropriated funds. To date, BIA-OJS has provided funding for: 25 Tribal Judges, 20 Tribal Prosecutors, 15 Tribal Defenders, 5 Tribal Guardians ad-Litem and provided funding for training and technical assistance for tribal court support staff as well as training for litigators in tribal courts.

Based upon the need to eradicate illegal narcotics in Indian Country, BIA-OJS was tasked with the responsibility, in coordination with the Attorney General, to ensure that BIA-OJS and tribal law enforcement as well as judicial personnel have access to training regarding the investigation and prosecution of offenses relating to illegal narcotics and alcohol and substance abuse prevention treatment. Since 2011, BIA-OJS has conducted 20 Tribal Court Trial Advocacy Training sessions which provide hands-on mock trial court training by skilled litigators including: federal prosecutors (AUSAs), tribal prosecutors (including those cross designated as SAUSAs), as well as federal defenders and tribal defenders.

To date, over 600 tribal court personnel have been trained on illegal narcotics and domestic violence prosecution, as well as prosecution of sexual assault crimes as identified under TLOA in Section 241 and 262.

These training sessions include discussions regarding the specific TLOA enhanced sentencing provisions. Moreover, BIA-OJS is working with the Department of Justice and the Administrative Office for U.S. Courts to better coordinate specialized training for those tribal court personnel ready to participate in the TLOA enhanced sentencing provisions under the Indian Civil Rights Act.

Since 2011, BIA-OJS has provided over 75 state of the art recording devices to tribal courts in an effort to comply with the requirement that all tribal courts implementing TLOA must record criminal proceedings. Further, BIA-OJS has provided funding allowing tribal courts to impose alternative sentences. For example, alcohol ankle bracelet monitoring programs have been used to reduce incarceration and address the severity of alcohol-related crimes. In 2012, the Lower Brule Sioux Tribe in South Dakota reported a 98% success rate against reoffending in instances where the devices were used. BIA-OJS is also coordinating with DOJ and IHS to work on providing training for tribal judges on alternative sentencing options.

Under TLOA, Tribes located in PL 280 states, where jurisdiction is the primary responsibility of the State, have the opportunity to request the federal government assume concurrent jurisdiction over certain crimes on the tribe's reservation. Some Tribes requesting concurrent jurisdiction have received tribal court assessments. The Department has provided funding to assist those tribal courts with addressing infrastructure stability which is essential for enhanced sentencing purposes, such as drafting criminal codes and rules of evidence, making rules of criminal procedures available to the public, providing qualified legal counsel to defendants, employing law trained judges and recording any criminal proceedings.

Corrections/Treatment

TLOA also sets forth requirements to address incarceration and substance use disorders in Indian Country. Section 211(b) of TLOA directed BIA-OJS to develop a long term plan for tribal detention programs.

To be responsive to this, the BIA published a plan for tribal detention programs in August 2011. Additionally, the BIA Corrections Handbook, First Edition, was developed and implemented in February of 2012. The handbook includes detailed policy and procedures that support the BIA Detention Guidelines and OJS has implemented these standards throughout the years. BIA-OJS continues to provide additional technical assistance to Tribes for the start-up and activation of newly constructed facilities, negotiating contracts with state and local jails for adult and juvenile bed space, inspection and certification processes, corrective action plan implementation, and assistance with grant applications.

Section 241 of TLOA identified the need for training on alcohol and substance use prevention and treatment and identified a mission of eradicating criminal acts caused by alcohol and substance use. In response, BIA-OJS created the Diversion and Re-entry Division (DRD) within the Tribal Justice Support Directorate. The purpose of the new Division was to transform current institutional practices and create alternatives to incarceration which build on existing treatment service continuums in tribal communities, as well as provide access to long-term detention-based treatment for all direct-service tribes at Hardin, Montana, Yuma, Arizona and Casper, Wyoming. These facilities are outstanding treatment and recovery resources for tribes that fill a critical need in Indian Country, expanding the overall continuum of services directly available to tribes.

The focus of the BIA-OJS initiative is to effectively braid opportunities and services of other federal agencies to address alcohol and substance use-related offenses. Importantly, BIA-OJS has worked with tribal courts and correctional facilities to administer a nationally recognized screening and assessment instrument (GAIN). The instrument is currently at three pilot sites and BIA-OJS has provided the training needed to administer the instrument. This instrument and new protocol for offender placement into service, service engagement and preparation for community re-entry services has the potential for serving as the cornerstone for linking all human service elements within tribal communities onto a common data infrastructure. BIA-OJS will generate a detailed analysis and year-end report of the Recidivism Reduction Initiative that includes a predictive analysis of the risk for offender recidivism, and will serve the need for a common data infrastructure within Indian Country.

Conclusion

Thank you for holding this hearing on the Tribal Law and Order Act and for providing the opportunity to discuss what we have done over the past five years since TLOA's enactment into law. We will continue to work closely with our Tribal, Federal, and State partners to address public safety issues in Indian Country and to further fulfill the goals of TLOA.

I am available to answer any questions the Committee may have.

Testimony of

Mirtha Beadle, MPA

Director, Office of Tribal Affairs and Policy

Substance Abuse and Mental health Services Administration

U. S. Department of Health and Human Services

Hearing on

Tribal Law and Order Act: Five Years Later: How have the Justice Systems in Indian Country Improved?

December 2, 2015

Chairman Barrasso, Ranking Member Tester, and members of the Senate Committee on Indian Affairs, thank you for inviting me to testify at this important hearing on the implementation of the Tribal Law and Order Act of 2010 (TLOA). I am pleased to testify along with colleagues from the Department of Interior (DOI) and Department of Justice (DOJ). Substance use is one of the most severe public health and safety problems facing American Indian and Alaska Native (AI/AN) individuals, families, and communities, and we must continue to work together to diminish the devastating social, economic, physical, mental, and spiritual consequences.

TLOA amended the Indian Alcohol and Substance Abuse Treatment Act of 1986 (Pub. L. 99-570). The amendments called for the Substance Abuse and Mental Health Services Administration (SAMHSA) to establish an office tasked with improving coordination among the federal agencies and departments responsible for combating alcohol and substance use disorders among the AI/AN population.[1] TLOA also instructs the Department of Health and Human Services (HHS) to collaborate with DOI and DOJ on determining the scope of ongoing problems; identifying resources and programs that would be relevant to combating alcohol and substance use disorders in tribal communities; and coordinating existing agency programs. Today, I am pleased to share with you the myriad ways in which SAMHSA, along with its federal partners and in coordination and consultation with tribal governments and organizations, is implementing the letter and spirit of the TLOA amendments.

---

[1] While the TLOA refers to alcohol and substance use among the AI/AN population, alcohol is a powerful substance itself. Given this distinction, this testimony will discuss this issue in terms of the prevention of alcohol and drug use and treatment of alcohol and substance use disorders.

Office of Indian Alcohol and Substance Abuse

As required by TLOA, SAMHSA established the Office of Indian Alcohol and Substance Abuse (OIASA) in 2010. OIASA was originally established within the Center for Substance Abuse Prevention, and in 2015 was realigned as a component of SAMHSA's new Office of Tribal Affairs and Policy (OTAP). SAMHSA's OTAP serves as the primary point of contact for tribal governments, tribal organizations, Federal departments and agencies, and other governments and agencies on behavioral health issues facing AI/AN populations. The creation of OTAP brought together SAMHSA's tribal affairs, tribal policy, tribal consultation, tribal advisory, and Tribal Law and Order Act (TLOA) responsibilities to improve agency coordination and achieve meaningful progress. As a component of OTAP, OIASA has greater reach across SAMHSA's centers and offices and is fully engaged in tribal policy and consultation efforts.

I'm pleased to mention that Marcella Ronyak, the OIASA Director, is at the hearing with me today. OIASA has three additional staff positions, including a permanent Indian Youth Programs Officer. To date, OIASA, along with our Federal partners – Indian Health Service (IHS), DOI, and DOJ - the Indian Alcohol and Substance Abuse Interdepartmental

Coordinating Committee (IASA Committee) has served as a point of contact for Indian Tribes with respect to the implementation of TLOA and finalized the Indian Alcohol and Substance Abuse Memorandum of Agreement as a framework for coordinating the resources and programs of SAMHSA, IHS, DOI, and DOJ, as directed by TLOA.

IASA Committee

For the past four years, the IASA Committee has served as an interagency forum for Federal partners to collaboratively work to support AI/AN communities in achieving their goals in the prevention, intervention, and treatment of alcohol and substance use disorders. The committee is composed of representatives from Federal agencies with responsibilities for addressing the consequences of alcohol and drug use in Indian Country, including SAMHSA, IHS, DOI's Bureau of Indian Affairs (BIA) and Bureau of Indian Education (BIE), and DOJ. The Director of OIASA serves as the Committee Chairperson. In addition, the Administration for Children and Families (ACF), Centers for Disease Control and Prevention (CDC), Centers for Medicare and Medicaid Services (CMS), Health Resources and Services Administration (HRSA), and National Institutes of Health (NIH) - all within HHS - and the White

House Office of National Drug Control Policy (ONDCP) are invited to attend IASA Committee meetings.

The IASA Committee work has and continues to focus on: (1) determining the scope of Indian alcohol and substance use problems; (2) advancing development of comprehensive tribal action planning; (3) identifying opportunities and programs relevant to alcohol and drug use among Tribal communities; (4) sharing information on practices, programs, and resources through the Prevention and Recovery Newsletter; and (5) addressing issues of concern to Tribes related to alcohol and drug use. The IASA Committee includes seven workgroups: (1) Memorandum of Agreement (MOA); (2) Tribal Action Plan; (3) Inventory/Resources; (4) Communications; (5) Native Youth Educational Services; (6) Data; and (7) Minimum Program Standards. Recently, the IASA Committee voted to establish a Public Safety and Health Workgroup to further enhance collaborations and actions related to re-entry services specific to youth regional treatment and detention centers, model juvenile code, and implementation of law enforcement and judicial personnel training, among other MOA responsibilities. Each of the workgroups is chaired by a TLOA Federal partner agency.

Memorandum of Agreement (MOA)

In fiscal year (FY) 2015, the MOA Workgroup initiated a significant effort to unify the TLOA and Indian Health Care Improvement Act (IHCIA) MOAs. Both MOAs address Indian alcohol and substance use and engage similar Federal partners in accomplishing requirements. The purpose of the unification effort is to identify areas of overlap and similarity between the two agreements and pave the way for greater coordination across Federal agencies. The MOA Workgroup is co-chaired by DOJ and IHS. OTAP developed background documents and an initial draft of a unified TLOA and IHCIA MOA for consideration. MOA Workgroup representatives have provided important input and recommendations not only for unifying the TLOA and ICHIA MOAs but also for streamlining and clarifying existing processes. Moving forward, the MOA Workgroup will provide leadership in the required annual review of the MOA.

Tribal Action Planning (TAP)

A primary focus of the IASA Committee is to advance comprehensive tribal action planning so that tribes can identify resources, priorities, and design a systems approach to treating alcohol and substance use disorders and their co-occurring conditions. The intent of coordinated

Federal TAP is to provide guidance, direction, coordination, and improved access for tribes to appropriate Federal resources that may assist them in developing and implementing tribal action plans. The TAP Workgroup coordinates support for tribes that choose to develop a TAP to prevent and treat alcohol and substance use disorders. The Workgroup has established a protocol for tribal requests for assistance and works with partner agency regional staff to coordinate assistance and resources for tribes in their areas.

In FY 2015, Tribal Action Plan trainings were held in four different geographic areas, reaching 44 tribes and 372 tribal participants. SAMHSA is leading the effort, in collaboration with Federal partners, to develop a new TAP strategy to advance comprehensive tribal action planning.

Engagement and Outreach on Indian Alcohol and Substance Abuse Issues

Within SAMHSA, OIASA has actively engaged with staff from the Center for Substance Abuse Prevention, Center for Substance Abuse Treatment, the Center for Mental Health Services, and the Center for Behavioral Health Statistics and Quality. OIASA also has provided updates and sought advice from the SAMHSA Tribal Technical Advisory Committee, which is composed of 14 elected/appointed tribal leaders.

Reaching far and wide to the tribal community, OIASA staff and I, as the OTAP Director, have attended, presented, and participated in tribal consultations and meetings in partnership with DOI, DOJ and IHS staff and leadership. OIASA also conducted outreach to national AI/AN organizations, such as the National Indian Health Board (NIHB), the National Congress of American Indians (NCAI), and the National Council of Urban Indian Health (NCUIH). In addition, OIASA has engaged with AI/AN stakeholders including Tribal Epidemiology Centers and tribal behavioral health staff.

SAMHSA's efforts to address alcohol and substance use are supported through several technical assistance (TA) centers and providers. The TA centers most pertinent to supporting alcohol and substance use prevention in AI/AN communities include:

- The Tribal Training and Technical Assistance Center, which provides TA on an array of tribal behavioral health and wellness needs and is the primary TA provider for tribal action planning;

- The National AI/AN Addiction Technology Transfer Center, which supports substance use disorder and other training to behavioral health providers and individuals from tribal communities; and

- The National Native Children's Trauma Center, which provides trainings and consultations to community agencies, tribal programs, clinicians, school personnel, technicians, and families on the impacts and prevention of childhood traumatic stress.

OIASA and Federal partners have actively worked to share information about programs and resources on alcohol and substance use prevention, intervention, and treatment with tribes and tribal organizations. The primary modalities are published on the TLOA Implementation website (http://www.samhsa.gov/tloa/) and Prevention and Recovery Newsletter. The website includes resources for developing tribal action plans, addressing issues faced by Native youth, and an inventory of Federal resources that may benefit tribes. The inventory was specifically developed in response to TLOA and includes over 70 Federally-sponsored education and alcohol and substance use prevention support programs; funding opportunity interactive links subdivided by HHS, DOI, and DOJ agencies and TLOA-related topics (i.e., public safety, justice systems and alcohol and substance use, corrections and 5 correctional alternatives, violence against women, juvenile justice); and, links to grant and contract resources. Over the past four years, Federal partners have published 14 issues of the *Prevention and Recovery* Newsletter, which has been downloaded over 200,000 times.

SAMHSA Grant Program Alignment with TLOA

SAMHSA has made addressing the behavioral health of American Indians and Alaska Natives a priority. In FY 2014, Congress appropriated $5 million to support the new Tribal Behavioral Health Grant (TBHG) program. With this funding, SAMHSA funded 20 tribes or tribal organizations. Grantees such as the Selawik Village Council in Alaska, the Turtle Mountain Band of Chippewa Tribe in North Dakota, and the Pueblo of Nambe in New Mexico plan to incorporate evidence-based, culture-based, and practice-based strategies for tribal youth. Grantees are required to work across tribal suicide prevention, mental health, substance use prevention, and substance use disorder treatment programs to build positive behavioral health among youth. Grantees connect appropriate cultural practices, intervention services, care, and information with families, friends, schools, educational institutions, correctional systems, substance use programs, mental health programs, foster care systems, and other support organizations for tribal youth. Technical assistance is provided to grantees through SAMHSA's Tribal Technical Assistance Center to support their ability to achieve their goals.

The President's FY 2016 Budget for the TBHG program is $30 million, including $15 million in the Mental Health appropriation and $15 million in the Substance Abuse Prevention appropriation. This represents an increase over the FY 2015 Enacted Level of $10 million in the Mental Health appropriation and $15 million for a newly established line in the Substance Abuse Prevention appropriation. This funding supports Generation Indigenous, an initiative focused on removing possible barriers to success for Native youth. This initiative takes a comprehensive, culturally appropriate approach to help improve the lives and opportunities for Native youth. In addition to HHS, multiple departments, including the Departments of Interior, Education, Housing and Urban Development, Agriculture, Labor, and Justice, are working collaboratively with tribes to address issues facing Native youth. The FY 2016 Budget allows SAMHSA to expand activities that are critical to preventing substance use and promoting mental health and resiliency among youth in tribal communities.

The additional funding would expand the TBHG program to approximately 103 additional tribes and tribal entities. With the expansion of the TBHG program, SAMHSA aims to reduce substance use and the incidence of suicide attempts among tribal youth and to address behavioral health conditions which impact learning in Bureau of Indian Education-funded schools. The TBHG program will support mental health promotion and substance use prevention activities for high-risk tribal youth and their families, enhance early detection of mental and substance use disorders among tribal youth, and increase referral to treatment.

Conclusion

Thank you again for this opportunity to share with you the extensive efforts SAMHSA and its Federal partners are undertaking, in collaboration with the AI/AN community, in order to implement TLOA, and to reduce the impact of alcohol and drug use on AI/AN communities. I would be pleased to answer any questions that you may have.

Testimony of

Tracy Toulou

Director, Office of Tribal Justice

Hearing on

Tribal Law and Order Act: Five Years Later: How have the Justice
Systems in Indian Country Improved?

December 2, 2015

Chairman Barrasso, Vice-Chairman Tester, and Members of the
Committee:

I am honored to appear before you to discuss the implementation efforts
of the Department of Justice (the Department, or DOJ) to fulfill our
responsibilities as established in the Tribal Law and Order Act of 2010
(TLOA) and, ultimately, to improve public safety in Indian country. In
introducing this Act in April 2009, Chairman Dorgan illuminated some of
the hard realities faced by tribes in modern times, including:
astonishingly high rates of violence, criminal exploitation of complex and
sometimes confusing jurisdiction, and crippling limitations on the legal
authorities of tribal governments to ensure safety on their lands. The
introduction of TLOA included a charge to the federal government to
provide tribal governments with the tools they need to better protect

their communities, to live up to our treaty and trust obligations, and to be more accountable for our efforts to enhance public safety in Indian country. Thank you for the opportunity to provide an overview of the Department's efforts over the past five years to fulfill our responsibilities under this Act and honor our broader obligations to Indian country.

In October 2009, the Department held a listening session with tribal leaders to help guide and inform the Department's policies, programs, and activities affecting Indian country going forward. Our leadership recognized the need to swiftly and meaningfully improve our contributions to public safety in Indian country, and as a result of this listening session, launched a Department-wide initiative to enhance public safety in Indian country, which is ongoing. With the passage of TLOA in July 2010, the Department's initiative expanded to absorb new responsibilities and assumed a renewed sense of urgency. Our work to enhance public safety has been, and continues to be, shaped by our commitment to empower tribal governments; to improve coordination and collaboration at the federal, tribal, state, and local levels; and to be appropriately accountable for the work we do.

Empowering Tribal Governments

The Department views tribes as partners in ensuring public safety in Indian country and is committed to maximizing tribal control over tribal affairs. It is our belief, informed by experience, that challenges faced by tribes are generally best met by tribal solutions. In support of this commitment, and the government-to-government nature of our relationships with tribes, the Department has worked to fulfill its responsibilities under TLOA in a way that will ultimately empower tribes to operate with more autonomy.

In order to support law enforcement activity by tribal officials in Indian country, tribes require access to law enforcement databases. Under TLOA, the Department must ensure that tribal law enforcement officials have access to national crime information databases. The ability of tribes to fully engage in national criminal justice information sharing via state networks, which are the long-time conduit for such activities, has been dependent upon regulations, statutes, and policies of the states that may not consistently enable tribal participation. In order to improve access for tribes, the Department has established two new programs and partnered on a third.

First, the Justice Telecommunications System (JUST) program, which was launched in 2010, provided participating tribes with access to the National Crime Information Center (NCIC). This program is ongoing and currently serves 23 tribes. This program, as well as the other two programs to improve data base access, were the result of on-going, substantive dialog with tribal governments and law enforcement.

Second, the Department recently launched a more comprehensive access program based on feedback from tribes and lessons learned from the JUST program: the DOJ Tribal Access Program for National Crime Information (TAP). The TAP program, first announced in August 2015, is designed to provide access to CJIS services, including: Next Generation Identification (NGI); National Data Exchange (N-DEx); Law Enforcement Enterprise Portal (LEEP); National Crime Information Center (NCIC); National Instant Criminal Background Check System (NICS); and Nlets, the International Justice and Public Safety Network. Nlets is an interstate public safety network for the exchange of law enforcement, criminal justice, and public safety information owned by the states. Nlets supports inquiry into state databases, such as motor vehicle, driver's license, and criminal history, as well as inquiry into several federal databases, such as DEA's Drug Pointer Index, ICE's Law Enforcement Support Center, and

FAA's Aircraft Registration, and Canada's Canadian Police Information Center. With funding from the Office of Justice Programs' (OJP) Office of Sex Offender Sentencing, Monitoring, Apprehending, Registering, and Tracking (SMART), the TAP program has selected ten tribal participants to help provide user feedback on the training, technical assistance, equipment, and maintenance of this program. Early feedback has been very positive, and it is our intention to eventually make this program available to any interested tribe. We will continue to work with Congress for additional funding to more broadly deploy the program.

The TAP Program was the result of a 2014 working group, which consisted of representatives from the Departments of Justice and the Interior. From this same close collaboration, the Department partnered with Interior's Bureau of Indian Affairs Office of Justice Services (BIA-OJS) in a third program known as "BIA Purpose Code X," which gives tribes the ability through BIA-OJS to perform emergency name-based background checks for child placement purposes This is a crucial capability for tribal social service agencies seeking emergency placement of children in Indian country.

The Department of Justice has increased its efforts to support tribal governments that are exercising expanded sentencing authority rooted in TLOA. While TLOA properly does not require the Department to review or certify a tribe's use of enhanced felony sentencing authority or the status of a tribe's efforts to amend its codes and court processes to provide defendants with the due process protections described in TLOA, we have taken steps to help ensure that tribes interested in exercising enhanced sentencing authority have knowledge of and access to relevant resources. For example, OJP's Bureau of Justice Assistance's Tribal Civil and Criminal Legal Assistance Program has provided training and technical services to support tribal civil and criminal legal procedures, legal infrastructure enhancements, public education, and the development and enhancement of tribal justice systems. More specifically, training and technical services have included the following: indigent legal defense services; civil legal assistance; public defender services; and strategies for the development and enhancement of tribal court policies, procedures, and codes.

The provision of high-quality training to tribal representatives has been an area of increased activity within the Department since the passage of TLOA. The Department believes that ensuring access to quality training is a necessary element to bolstering tribal autonomy. In July 2010, the

Executive Office of U.S. Attorneys (EOUSA) launched the National Indian Country Training Initiative (NICTI) to ensure that federal prosecutors and agents, as well as state and tribal criminal justice personnel, receive the training and support needed to address the particular challenges relevant to Indian country prosecutions. Importantly, the Department covers the costs of travel and lodging for tribal attendees at classes sponsored by the NICTI. This allows many tribal criminal justice officials to receive cutting-edge training from national experts at no cost to the student or tribe. The NICTI has sponsored approximately 75 training courses, and reached over 200 tribal, federal, and state agencies.

Additionally, the Federal Bureau of Investigation (FBI) announced a forthcoming training course to be held at the FLETC campus in Artesia, New Mexico. Jointly taught by FBI and BIA "mentors" and FLETC common core instructors, the course will include instruction in forensic evidence collection and preparatory instruction on investigations common to Indian country, such as domestic violence, child abuse, violent crimes, human trafficking, and drug trafficking. This course will be held four times each year, with a total of 24 students in each session. This course, the result of collaboration between FBI, BIA, and FLETC, was developed out of a recognized need to train federal and tribal law enforcement officers together. Another recent training was held by DOJ's Drug Enforcement Administration (DEA). In September 2015, the National Native American Law Enforcement Association held a collaborative training event where the DEA provided on-site training on clandestine lab awareness for first responders, emerging technologies, and money laundering. The training included federal, state, local, and tribal partners with Indian country responsibility.

One of the most meaningful displays of the Department's commitment to a government-to-government relationship with tribes is in our efforts to cross-deputize tribal law enforcement officials. In doing so, we not only expand their authorities, but we send an important message that we are partners and allies with tribes in our collective efforts to enhance public safety in Indian country. The Special Assistant U.S. Attorney (SAUSA) Program was developed prior to the passage of TLOA to train tribal prosecutors in federal criminal law, procedure, and investigative techniques to increase prosecutions in federal court, tribal court, or both. The program enables tribal prosecutors to bring cases in federal court and to serve as co-counsel with federal prosecutors on felony investigations and prosecutions of offenses originating in tribal communities. The program has grown considerably since the passage of

TLOA. To date, there are 25 SAUSAs representing 23 tribes. In addition to the SAUSA program, DOJ investigative agencies have cross-deputized tribal law enforcement officers through joint task forces. For example, the FBI has deputized 85 tribal law enforcement officers as part of the Safe Trails Task Forces. There are currently 15 active Safe Trails Task Forces located around the country, working to combat violent crime, drugs, gangs, and gaming violations.

In 2014, the Bureau of Prisons (BOP) fulfilled a key provision of TLOA by accepting certain tribal offenders sentenced in tribal courts for placement in BOP institutions. The pilot program allowed any federally-recognized tribe to request that the BOP incarcerate a tribal member convicted of a violent crime under the terms of Section 234 of TLOA and authorized the BOP to house up to 100 tribal offenders at a time, nationwide.

A fundamental goal of the BOP is to reduce future criminal activity by encouraging inmates to participate in a range of programs that have been proven to help them adopt a crime-free lifestyle upon their return to the community. Through the pilot program, tribal offenders have access to the BOP's many self-improvement programs, including work in prison industries and other institution jobs, vocational training, education, treatment for substance use disorders, classes on parenting and anger management, counseling, religious observance opportunities and other programs that teach essential life skills. BOP has also ensured that there are culturally-appropriate offerings for native inmates. In addition to increasing access to critical programs and treatments, the pilot program facilitated tribes' ability to exercise enhanced sentencing authority under TLOA, which is an important indication of support for tribal sovereignty. The pilot program was, by all accounts, a success, and both tribes and the Department would be supportive of necessary Congressional action to reauthorize this program.

An important part of our support to tribes is necessarily tied to funds. The Department launched the Coordinated Tribal Assistance Solicitation (CTAS) in 2010, as a response to tribes' request for increased flexibility. Through CTAS, tribes and tribal consortia are able to submit a single application to apply for a broad range of DOJ tribal grant programs. Through CTAS, the Department has awarded over 1,400 grants totaling more than $620 million. Over time, we have refined this solicitation to enable tribes to take a truly comprehensive approach to improving public safety in tribal communities. Under TLOA, the Department was required to offer specific grants for delinquency prevention and response, and to include dedicated funding for regional information sharing. To date, we have awarded more than $44 million in support of tribal youth programs and more than $108 million to support regional information sharing systems. The Department continually seeks feedback from tribes on ways to improve CTAS, and each year with our solicitation announcement we also communicate steps we have taken during the previous year to improve the process. The most recent solicitation was released on November 19, 2015, with an application deadline of February 23, 2016. It incorporates a number of changes, including the elimination of certain eligibility requirements, broadening allowable activities, and extending the award period for certain grants. Each year, the intention is to increase the accessibility and usefulness of CTAS grants.

In parallel to our outward-facing efforts, the Department has made a number of internal structural changes to ensure our revamped presence in Indian country is long-lived.

Evolution of Agency Infrastructure

To ensure that the day-to-day operations at the Department are supportive of the policy and programmatic changes we have made since the passage of TLOA, we have made a number of internal adjustments across the Department, from headquarters to field offices. The intent in making these changes was to absorb the principles that drive the TLOA and our response to that Act, thus integrating them into the way we do business at the Department. Indeed, although not a direct response to TLOA, the Department issued Attorney General Guidelines Stating Principles for Working with Federally Recognized Tribes (Statement of Principles) in December 2014 to guide and inform all of the Department's interactions with federally-recognized tribes. This Statement of Principles serves as a point of reference for Department employees and, importantly, a standard to which tribes can hold the Department accountable.

In 1995, then-Attorney General Janet Reno established the Office of Tribal Justice (OTJ). OTJ has operated continuously since then, although it was not made permanent until the passage of TLOA. On November 17, 2010, less than four months after TLOA's enactment, the Department published in the *Federal Register* a final rule that established OTJ as a permanent, standalone component of the Department. My office serves as a principal point of contact in the Department for federally-recognized tribes, provides legal, policy, and programmatic advice to the Attorney General with respect to the treaty and trust relationship between the

United States and Indian tribes, promotes internal uniformity of Department policies and litigation positions relating to Indian country, and coordinates with other Federal agencies and with State and local governments on their initiatives in Indian country.

The U.S. Attorneys' Offices with Indian country in their districts play a primary role in our interactions with tribes. U.S. Attorneys' Offices often are the nexus of activity when federal involvement on reservations is necessary, from investigations to prosecutions to providing services to victims. Every U.S Attorney's Office, whose district includes Indian country or a federally-recognized tribe, has at least one Tribal Liaison, and some districts have more than one. Along with the TLOA-driven requirement that each relevant office appoint a Tribal Liaison, the U.S. Attorneys are required to hold annual consultations with tribes in their districts. In order to assist the U.S. Attorney's Offices and the Attorney General's Advisory Committee's Native American Issues Subcommittee, as well as to serve as a liaison to other DOJ components, the Executive Office for U.S. Attorneys formally established the position of Native American Issues Coordinator.

These changes to the structure of the Department were driven by the Department's support for and fulfillment of its responsibilities under TLOA. There have been a series of policy shifts that are not a direct response to the Act but are in keeping with the spirit of that legislation. For example, the issuance of the DOJ Statement of Principles, discussed earlier, marks an important shift in our approach at all levels of the Department to interacting with tribes. Similarly, the DOJ Consultation Policy is based on three guiding principles: that the Department must engage with tribal nations on a government-to-government basis; that tribal sovereignty and Indian self-determination are now, and must always be, the foundations of every policy or program; and that communication and coordination with our tribal partners, among federal agencies, and with our state and local counterparts are essential to accountability and to success.

Greater Accountability

Accountability is a critical element in a true partnership, and the Department has taken a number of steps to increase our accountability to tribes. The TLOA-mandated reports were intended to promote greater transparency of Department activities in Indian country, and the process of responding has been a useful exercise for our agency to scrutinize trends and patterns of activity. In some cases, the reports have revealed a need to expand our agency response to meet specific needs and organize our resources more effectively, such as those related to long-term detention. In other cases, the reporting process highlighted positive impacts that Department activity has had in Indian country over time and a need to perpetuate beneficial initiatives, such as the BOP pilot program report and the Office of Community Oriented Policing Services (COPS) Report. In tracking prosecutions and crime data, the Department has benefitted from taking a focused look at our response to trends in Indian country, and as a result is in a better position to adjust our resources internally to address emerging trends and issues.

The Department has made progress over the past five years in bolstering our government-to-government relationship with tribes and in honoring our treaty and trust obligations. We are all fully cognizant that there is significant work still to be done to live up to our responsibilities in Indian country, and we are committed to seeing this work through. We appreciate Congress' efforts to foster public safety, and look forward to working closely with our partners in Indian country to fully honor our responsibilities. I will be happy to answer any questions you may have.

Prepared Statement of

Glen G. Gobin

Vice Chairman the Tulalip Tribes

Hearing on

Tribal Law and Order Act: Five Years Later: How have the Justice Systems in Indian Country Improved?

December 2, 2015

Good afternoon Chairman Barrasso, Vice-Chairman Tester, and Committee Members, my name is Glen Gobin, Vice-Chairman of the Tulalip Tribes. I would like to thank you for the opportunity to testify on the Tribal Law and Order Act and its effect on criminal justice systems in Indian Country.

Introduction

The Tulalip Tribes are the successors in interest to the Snohomish, Snoqualmie, Skykomish, and a number of allied bands, who have occupied the Puget Sound region in Washington State since time immemorial, and were signatory to the 1855 Treaty of Point Elliot. Under the terms of the treaty, these tribes moved to the Tulalip Indian

Reservation and in 1934 under the Indian Reorganization Act, chose to use the name the "Tulalip Tribes" which is named for a bay on the Reservation.

We thank the committee for supporting the Tribal Law and Order Act of 2010 in an effort to better address crime in Indian County. The purpose of the Tribal Law and Order Act (TLOA) is to make US Attorney and federal agencies more accountable for serving Native communities, to provide greater authority and autonomy to Tribal Nations to operate their own justice systems and protect their communities, and to enhance cooperation between federal and state officials in law enforcement training and access to criminal justice information. Although Tribal justice systems still face significant jurisdictional and funding obstacles, the TLOA is a positive, initial step forward in providing tribal justice systems with increased authority and tools needed to keep tribal communities safe.

Tulalip initially expanded its justice system in 2001 when it retroceded criminal jurisdiction from the State of Washington. In the last decade, the Tulalip justice system has made great strides, developing a full service police department and court system as well a strong support system of prosecutors, probation officers and public defenders.

During the same period, Tulalip incorporated Quil Ceda Village (Village) to promote Reservation based business development. The success of this economic development has created thousands of new jobs and brought in millions of new visitors to the Reservation. However, our government is still unable to collect the necessary taxes to support critical governmental functions that other state, federal and local governments enjoy. The imposition, assessment, and collection of taxes by the state and county undermine and prevent Tulalip and the Village from exercising its own sovereign taxing authority. As a direct result, the tribes must subsidize and finance, with millions of tribal hard dollars each year, the necessary governmental infrastructure and services to the Village businesses. The end result, is that the Tribes cannot devote those revenues to the needs of the tribal community, including its criminal justice system. Although it has been difficult to expand the justice system to cover these increased responsibilities with finite tribal resources, a strong public safety system is vital for the continued growth of the Tulalip community. Much of the recent success Tulalip has had would not have been possible without an effective tribal justice system that community members, visitors and businesses can rely on.

After the passage of the TLOA, Tulalip amended its criminal codes to increase sentencing authority for major felony crimes. As other tribes experienced, these amendments took time to expand the corresponding infrastructure needs. In 2014, Tulalip requested to participate and was chosen for the VAWA Special Domestic Violence Court Jurisdiction Pilot Project, and today we continue to prosecute non-natives for domestic violence crimes. Since that time we have had 11 cases, with 6 convictions, 2 dismissals, 1 transferred to the US Attorney's office and 2 pending. Under the VAWA tribal provisions, domestic violence crimes can be designated as crimes subject to TLOA enhanced sentencing guidelines. Furthermore, pursuant to the TLOA, with the support of the Executive U.S. Attorney's office and after many discussions with the Western District U.S. Attorney, one of our Tulalip tribal prosecutors is designated as a Special Assistant U.S. Attorney (SAUSA) to prosecute reservation crimes in federal court. This SAUSA appointment has improved collaboration and communication between our respective agencies, resulting in increased prosecutions of sexual predators.

Since Tulalip received retrocession and years prior to implementing greater criminal justice authority under the TLOA, it has been committed to protecting the rights of the accused. All of the Tulalip judges, prosecutors and criminal defense lawyers are highly qualified attorneys. Tulalip provides all indigent defendants with legal counsel without charge. All basic rights of defendants are recognized and codified into the Tulalip criminal justice codes. All defendants have the right to appeal to the Tulalip Court of Appeals. Just as important, the Tulalip court is best suited to address crime and impose sentences in a culturally appropriate way, which includes exploring alternatives that help offenders, victims and the community heal. As a result of this robust justice system and increased jurisdictional authority, we have seen an increase in victims coming forward to report crimes as they are seeing that their perpetrators will be held accountable.

There is no question that the Tribal Law and Order Act has enabled Tulalip to better protect its community. Although the TLOA still leaves the tribes reliant on federal prosecution for most serious crimes, even with the addition of another tribal liaison as TLOA authorized, the U.S. Attorney will still decline to prosecute some major offenses for a variety of reasons. In these situations, it is vital for the Tribal court to have the authority and capacity to appropriately sentence violent offenders. Under the TLOA enhanced sentencing guidelines, Tulalip has filed approximately 33 charges carrying a sentence of more than one year. Federal and state prosecutors are often unwilling to pursue domestic violence and sexual assault cases on the Reservation because they are time consuming and inherently difficult to prosecute. The TLOA enhanced sentencing guidelines have proven especially useful as a tool for addressing these crimes on the Tulalip Reservation. We have one person convicted of rape of a child and is serving three years (the max available) in federal prison, through the Bureau of Prisons Pilot Project.

The Tulalip Tribes values its relationship with the U.S. Attorney's Office, which has been an important partner in fighting crime on the Reservation. The provisions of the TLOA providing for better reporting and communication between the U.S. Attorney's Office and Indian tribes have proved helpful in improving this relationship. Since the passage of the TLOA, Tulalip prosecutors have developed a better working relationship with the Assistant U.S. Attorneys in the Seattle Office, and the Tulalip Police Department has forged a better relationship with federal law enforcement.

While in the Tribal Law and Order Act of 2010 Congress required the Attorney General to ensure that tribal agencies that met applicable requirements be permitted access to national crime information databases, the ability of tribes to fully participate in national criminal justice information sharing via state networks has been dependent upon various regulations, statutes and policies of the states in which a tribe's land is located. The Washington State Patrol is the CSA for the state, and it is also the administrator for the state database. Under Washington law, the Tulalip Tribes access to the national crime information databases has been limited that at times endangers officer safety and our community at large. For example our tribal court domestic violence protection orders were not directly entered into the database. Instead we had to through a state intermediary, which introduced extra layers of bureaucracy that introduced delays, errors, and sometimes prevented orders from being entered into NCIC-POF. Earlier this year, we began participation in the JUST pilot project and last month we were notified that we will be included in the User face of the Tribal Access Program (TAP).

Despite the recent progress, Indian Country continues to face a crisis of violent crime. A Bureau of Justice Statistics Report covering the period 1992-2002 found that American Indians are victims of violent crime a rate more than **twice** that of the national population. *"American Indians and Crime." (U.S. DOJ Publication No. NCJ 203097).Washington, DC: U.S. Department of Justice (2004).* According to the DOJ-BJS report, American Indians experienced an estimated 1 violent crime for every 10 residents over age 12. The figures are even worse for Native American women, who are the victims of rape or sexual assault at a rate more than 2.5 times that of American women in general. The DOJ- BJS study concluded that 34.1 percent of American Indian and Alaska Native women - more than one in three - will be raped in their lifetime. The enactment of the Tribal Law and Order Act was an important step toward dealing with crime in Indian country, but much still needs to be done. Checkerboard jurisdiction and lack of tribal criminal justice authority over most non-Indian offenders create unnecessary obstacles to addressing Reservation crime. The need to build upon TLOA and the VAWA tribal provisions is critical as we move forward. For example, in 6 of our 11 SDVCJ cases, children were present and victims of crime. Other Pilot Project tribes experienced the same phenomena; even where the law has been implemented, tribal prosecutors are limited in their authority and cannot charge an offender who simultaneously abuses or endangers his children, commits a drug or alcohol offense or property crime, interferes with the reporting of the domestic violence, or who physically or sexually assaults someone other than an intimate partner. Of our six child victims only one will have its crime redressed because the case is in the federal system.

Criminal cases are best handled by local law enforcement, which is tribal law enforcement on the Indian reservation. Tulalip police officers all possess both tribal and Washington State general peace officer commissions with authority to arrest under tribal and state laws. At Tulalip, the Tribal police department responds to all police calls on the Reservation, from both the Indian and non-Indian community. Incidents range from simple misdemeanors to major crimes such as murder and rape. In 2015, Tribal law enforcement has made a total of 835 arrests. Roughly 60 % of the arrestees were non-Indian. Tribal criminal justice systems need full jurisdiction, with federal assistance, to prosecute persons arrested by local law enforcement in order to truly keep their communities safe.

The Tulalip Tribes remain committed to operating an excellent and effective justice system. The same principles of accountability and fairness recognized in the United States justice system are equally important in the Tribal justice systems. However, criminal justice requires substantial and reliable sources of revenues to operate effectively.

The increased responsibility Tulalip has taken on in addressing crime has strained tribal budgets. Police, courts, indigent defense and probation all require significant levels of funding. The expense of incarceration is one of the highest hurdles for Tribes to implement the enhanced sentencing authority under the TLOA. Furthermore, prosecuting cases in which a defendant may face up to three years in custody carries higher costs, as there will be greater prosecution and defense expenses, as well as longer trials. In addition, these defendants have a higher need for appropriate re-entry programs as these crimes are more severe and the perpetrator needs more reeducation and treatment to return to the tribal community. Tribal governments must balance these needs with other important unmet needs such as housing, education and health care for the Indian community.

Providing tribal courts with greater authority will not be effective unless the federal government steps up and supports Indian tribes with equal funding and removes limitations to our authority to generate new revenues. States and other local governments have greater direct access to federal funding resources that tribes either cannot access, or the barriers are so great to access, that attempt to obtain the funding is pointless because of barriers or conditions that a state places on tribes. A prime example of unequal funding is the recent increase that states are receiving from the Victims of Crime Act, in which the state of Washington funding is increased from around 3 million to over 35 million for this year. There is no mandated tribal set aside or formal system for meaningful consultation for tribes to benefit from this funding. VOCA provides no meaningful tribal set aside. We have been encouraged by the introduction of the SURVIVE Act, but passage is still uncertain. Increased federal funding is necessary for Tribes to build capacity and operate justice systems effectively. We call upon the federal government to actively support Tribal governments in their efforts to gain greater authority to raise revenues through tribal taxation in order to meet criminal justice and other important tribal government responsibilities. We also call for equality in access to all justice system funding programs with a mandated tribal set-aside that goes directly through to the tribes.

Specific Amendments Needed to TLOA

- <u>The Bureau of Prison program</u>.

The Bureau of Prisons Tribal Prisoner Program should be expanded, streamlined, and made permanent to include other non-violent TLOA and VAWA crimes that qualify for enhanced sentencing. The Bureau of Prison project was a 3.5 year program; however, it took a minimum of 2 years for many tribes to enact TLOA. Furthermore, use of the BOP project was limited to sentencing of 2 years and 1 day, and limited to violent crimes. Thus, few tribes were able to utilize the BOP project and it soon went away. The BOP program needs to be expanded so that tribes can utilize these jail facilities for sentencing of over 1 year and 1 day similar to other criminal justice agencies. In addition, Defendants convicted on Special Domestic Violence Court Jurisdiction (SDVCJ) should be included as eligible defendants as well as repeat violators of DV protection orders and stalking crimes. As the process currently exists, violations of protection orders and stalking crimes are not characterized as violent crimes for purposes of BOP Pilot Project participation criteria. Such a narrow view does not recognize that these types of crimes can be just as lethal or impactful as "violent" crimes. The process could be streamlined and less burdensome than the past application process.

The value of this program goes beyond the obvious one of not having the tribe bear the expense of longer-term incarceration. In addition, use of this program can be used as a prosecutor tool. There are times when we have a case that could possibly be filed by the USAO, but that we feel is more appropriately addressed in Tribal Court. One circumstance is when we feel it's important to the community, for a variety of reasons, to have justice done here at Tulalip. Sometimes the conduct is egregious enough that two, three, or more years seems called for, but if filed in federal court could result in 30 years – essentially life in prison in some cases. In addition, we might have a case that really *should* be prosecuted by the USAO, but for some reason they are not willing to take the case. In those instances we can offer a significant sentence, but the financial burden on the Tribes would be extreme. Perhaps the most important benefit to the Tribes is that a sentence served in federal prison removes the defendant from the community. Inmates have much less influence on community members and vice-versa. You can see how a person operating a criminal enterprise of some kind could continue to do so if s/he had regular contact with people on the outside. Similarly, DV victims would be more easily intimidated and manipulated if visitation were possible. Furthermore, a county jail such as the one utilized by our Tribe is really intended for much shorter-term incarceration, and offers much less in the way of rehabilitative services to inmates that might affect future behavior and reduce recidivism. Our Tribe only became TLOA-qualified and VAWA-qualified in the last two years. It is anticipated that as this enhanced jurisdiction is asserted more and more over time, the option of sending our prisoners to federal prison could be utilized more and more.

- NCIC/criminal databases and Tribal Access.

The Tulalip Tribes urges the appropriation of financial resources towards fully implementing the Tribal Access Program (TAP) to Federal Databases. The TAP program will need to be fully funded as a permanent program in partnership with Indian Tribes to enhance delivery to tribal governments and provide ongoing improvements while keeping all interested tribes informed of the delivery of this program. The Tulalip Tribes is honored to be selected as a Pilot project tribe for TAP, but it is potentially already encountering unnecessary limitations because there is insufficient funding for our defined need to fully utilize the program thus databases, as other non-tribal governments are able to do.

Conclusion

Thank you for taking the time to listen to our concerns, the voices and needs of our tribe, and for considering our recommendations. We believe in the continuation of building alliances to enhance and promote the needs of tribal justice agencies. By working together we stand stronger in our advocacy efforts for equal access to justice, local based solutions to local problems, and access to services and advocacy designed by and for Native communities.